ISBN 0 86112 806 0
© Brimax Books Ltd 1985
All rights reserved.
Brimax Paperbacks edition first published 1990
Brimax Paperbacks is an imprint of Brimax Books Ltd,
Newmarket, England
Printing in Great Britain by
The Eagle Press plc, Glasgow

DRAGON and THE RABBITS

BY LUCY KINCAID

ILLUSTRATED BY ERIC KINCAID

BRIMAX PAPERBACKS

Dragon lives in the wood.
He hums songs with the bees.
The baby rabbits want to hum too. They do not know how to hum.

What are they doing?

crying

hopping

peeping

hiding

listening